AF407159

Zero to Hero in Real Estate

*The Ultimate Guide for
the Over-40 Investor*

By Rovan Deon

Copyright © 2024 by Rovan Deon

All rights reserved. No part of this publication may be reproduced, distributed or transmitted in any form or by any means, including photocopying, recording, or other electronic or mechanical methods, without the prior written permission of the author or publisher, except in the case of brief quotations embodied in critical reviews and certain other noncommercial uses permitted by copyright law.

This publication is designed to provide accurate and authoritative information about the subject matter covered. It's sold with the understanding that the author and publisher are not engaged in rendering legal, intellectual property, accounting, medical, psychological, or other professional advice. If legal advice or other professional assistance is required, the services of a competent professional should be sought. The author and publisher, individually or corporately, do not accept any responsibility for any liabilities resulting from the actions of any parties involved.

About the Author

International Best Selling Author Rovan Deon is a guiding light in the field of Transformational and Personal Development, with an illustrious career spanning over three decades. His journey has been characterized by a deep commitment to personal growth and development, both as a practitioner and an educator. Rovan Deon is certified by the State of New York as a real estate instructor and loves teaching everything about real estate. In 2024, Rovan's dedication to education and financial literacy education was recognized by the United Federation of Teachers with the prestigious Outstanding Educator Award for Career and Technical Education (CTE), highlighting over two decades of exceptional contributions to the field.

ZERO TO HERO IN REAL ESTATE

Rovan Deon's expertise is not confined to the classroom; his influence extends to the highest echelons of professional success. As a sought-after coach, he has guided a diverse clientele to achieve their fullest potential. His clients include individuals working for prestigious organizations such as the United Nations, as well as small business owners and entrepreneurs who have graced the pages of major magazines. His mentorship and coaching have been pivotal for vice presidents at some of the world's largest banks, educators, brain surgeons, and entertainers from ghostwriters to celebrities. Moreover, his guidance has touched the lives of lawyers, Grammy-nominated artists, filmmakers, and speechwriters for presidents as well as heads of states of Africa, showcasing his versatility and profound impact across various industries globally.

Beyond his professional achievements, Rovan Deon cherishes his personal life in New Jersey, where he resides with his beautiful wife, Adele, and their daughter, Jade. His life is a testament to the belief that, with the right guidance, individuals can not only envision success but also achieve it. Rovan Deon continues to inspire and empower, leaving an unforgettable mark on the lives of those he touches through his coaching and through his works.

Continue learning by purchasing other books by Rovan Deon, including **You Already Have IT - A** *Survival Guide To Life* and the **SO' HUM** **GRATEFUL JOURNAL** - *CREATE AN ATTITUDE OF GRATITUDE IN JUST 5 MIN A DAY* both available on Amazon!

Acknowledgement

To my dearest mom, Helen McGee,

As I sit down to pen this acknowledgment, words seem to fall short of expressing the gratitude and love I hold for you. You have been my unwavering support, my guiding light through the darkest of times, and the embodiment of unconditional love. From my very first breath, you have been my first love, teaching me the virtues of kindness, resilience, and compassion.

Your sacrifices have not gone unnoticed, Mom. The countless times you placed our needs above your own, prioritizing our happiness and well-being, are etched in my heart forever. You have mastered the art of selflessness, often putting yourself last to ensure we had everything we needed and more.

Your down-to-earth nature and authenticity have always been a source of comfort and strength. In a world filled with pretenses, your ability to remain true to yourself and to us has been a guiding star. You've always said that honesty is the foundation of trust, and your candidness, even when the truth was hard to bear, has been a valuable lesson in integrity and courage.

Mom, your strength is unparalleled. You've faced life's challenges with a grace and fortitude that inspire me daily. Your independence and beauty, both inside and out, have taught me the true meaning of self-worth and confidence.

As I share this book with the world, I do so with the knowledge that I could not have reached this point without your love, support, and belief in me. You have been my rock, my inspiration, and my greatest cheerleader. This achievement is as much yours as it is mine.

Thank you, Mom, for everything. For the love, the lessons, and the life you've given me. I am because you are.

In the journey of life and within the pages of this book, there are two extraordinary women whose influence and love have shaped not only the words herein, but the very essence of who I am. To my beloved wife, Adele Hill, and my cherished daughter, Jade Lauryn Hill, this acknowledgment is but a small tribute to the profound impact you have both had on my life.

To Adele, my partner, my anchor, and my inspiration—your wit, inherited from your father, brings laughter and light into our lives, making every day brighter. Your caring and loving nature envelops our family in warmth, making our home a sanctuary of peace and happiness. Your leadership, both gentle and firm, guides us, and your innovative ideas illuminate the path forward. Adele, you keep me grounded, reminding me of what truly matters in life. Your support and belief in me have been unwavering, a testament to the depth of your love and strength. I love you deeply and unreservedly, grateful every day for the blessing of walking this life's journey with you.

To Jade Lauryn Hill, my brilliant daughter, you are a beacon of hope and promise. Your intelligence, leadership, and the grace with which you embrace your own journey of growth and discovery fill me with pride. Jade, you give me a profound purpose to continue showing up in the world, to strive for excellence, and to be a role model worthy of your admiration. Watching you navigate life with such zest and wisdom is a constant reminder of the beautiful future that lies ahead. Daddy is beyond proud of you, inspired by your strength, your kindness, and the extraordinary person you are becoming.

This book is a milestone in a journey that I could not have embarked on without the two of you. Adele, your love and partnership are my foundation; Jade, your existence and spirit are my motivation. Together, you are my heart, my soul, and my everything.

To Oliver Ragsdale Jr., my mentor, my friend, my role model, and a father figure like no other,

This acknowledgment could never fully encapsulate the depth of gratitude and respect I have for you, yet it is a heartfelt attempt to honor the pivotal role you have played in my life. From my formative teenage years to the man I am today, your guidance, wisdom, and unwavering support have been my north star.

Oliver, you have been more than a mentor; you have been my saving grace in times of despair, the beacon of light guiding me through my darkest moments. Your belief in me never wavered, even when I struggled to believe in myself. You never gave up on me, instilling a sense of hope and courage that has become the bedrock of my existence.

Our adventures together are cherished memories, each one a lesson in living life to its fullest and embracing the joy in every moment. You taught me the value of true friendship and the importance of being there for one another, no matter the circumstances.

Your influence extends beyond the personal; it has shaped my professional aspirations and achievements. You gave me the courage to chase after my dreams, no matter how lofty, and to demand the very best from myself. Your example has shown me what it means to lead with integrity, passion, and determination.

Oliver, your presence in my life and the lives of my family members is a gift we hold dear. You continue to be the hero who shows up, time and again, with love, guidance, and an unwavering commitment to our well-being.

As I share this book with the world, I do so knowing that your teachings, your spirit, and your legacy are woven into its pages. You have helped shape the person I am today, and for that, I am eternally grateful.

In Memory of Malcolm Stevens,

In the pages of this book lies not just my journey as an author and educator but the essence of a mentorship that transcended the ordinary—Malcolm Stevens, you were more than a mentor; you were a beacon of inspiration, a friend whose wisdom and generosity knew no bounds.

Malcolm, with every hour we drove, every conversation we shared, you poured into me not just knowledge but a profound appreciation for education, life, and the arts. Your ability to see potential in me, long before I could see it in myself, has been the cornerstone of my growth, both personally and professionally. You were not just teaching; you were nurturing a vision in me that I was yet to discover.

Your dedication went beyond the call of duty; giving the shirt off your back was not just a metaphor but a testament to your boundless generosity. As a brilliant drama coach and counselor, you did not merely instruct you inspired, pushing me to explore the depths of my capabilities and to always strive for more. The full spectrum of the arts and the discipline you introduced me to has enriched my soul and broadened my horizons immeasurably.

The words 'giving up' were alien to your vocabulary. Your unwavering faith in my abilities and your relentless encouragement propelled me forward, even in moments of doubt. You were a force of nature, Malcolm, a champion for the potential within young people, igniting a fire that would drive us to reach our fullest potential.

Though you have passed on, your spirit remains a guiding light in my life. The lessons you imparted, the love you shared, and the path you paved for me and many others will resonate throughout generations. You are forever in my heart, Malcolm, and the legacy of your teachings continues to inspire not just me, but every young person I encounter. In carrying forward the wisdom you bestowed upon us, I hope to honor your memory and continue the work you so passionately believed in.

Even in your absence, my love for you endures. There isn't a day that goes by that doesn't remind me of the lessons you have taught me. This book is a celebration and also a tribute to you—a celebration of the impact you made on my life and the lives of many others. Malcolm, you were a true champion of the arts, education, and of the human spirit.

Contents

Introduction 1

Chapter 1: Understanding Real Estate Investing 4

Chapter 2: Getting Started with Real Estate Investing 18

Chapter 3: Market Analysis and Location Section 29

Chapter 4: Financial Fundamentals 38

Chapter 5: The Trinity Approach to Real Estate Valuation .. 47

Chapter 6: Real Estate Investment Strategies 54

Chapter 7: Risk Management In Real Estate Investing 67

Next Steps In Your Real Estate Investment Journey 75

The Golden Key – Zero to Hero in Real Estate Mindset 78

Introduction

Zero to Hero in Real Estate: The Ultimate Guide for the Over-40 Investor is more than just a guide; it's a beacon of hope and a testament to the timeless potential within each of us, regardless of age. This book stands as a powerful reminder that starting your journey in real estate investing after 40 is not just a possibility, but an opportunity for remarkable growth and success.

Imagine standing at a crossroads, with decades of life experience behind you and a future filled with untapped potential ahead. This is where you are now. It's a place of strength, wisdom, and resilience. In these pages, we celebrate these qualities, harnessing them to fuel your journey in real estate investing. You're not just learning about property and markets;

you're unlocking a new chapter of your life, one filled with financial freedom and personal achievement.

Each concept and strategy in this book is presented with the purpose of inspiring you to see beyond the conventional boundaries of age and time. It's about rewriting the narrative that says it's too late to start something new. You may have heard stories of real investors who began their real estate journey later in life and achieved incredible success. You'll see firsthand that your dreams are not just valid, but entirely achievable.

You're not simply reading a book; you're embarking on a transformative journey. The knowledge you gain here is a powerful tool, and the real magic lies in your ability to apply it. With every page, you'll feel more empowered, more confident, and more equipped to take on the world of real estate investing. This isn't just about securing financial stability; it's about building a legacy, creating something of lasting value, and proving to yourself and others that age is merely a number, not a limitation.

The purpose of *Zero to Hero in Real Estate: The Ultimate Guide for the Over-40 Investor* is to ignite a fire within you. It's to show you that now is your time to shine, to take the wealth of your life experiences and channel them into a successful real estate investment journey. This book is your compass, guiding you towards a future where financial freedom and personal fulfillment are not just aspirations but realities waiting to be claimed.

So, embrace this journey with an open heart and a determined spirit. The path to real estate mastery awaits you, and the best is yet to come. Let this book be your guide, your inspiration, and your stepping stone to a future where you are not just an investor but a hero in your own right, a true testament to the power of starting wherever you are and rising to heights you never thought possible.

CHAPTER 1

Understanding Real Estate Investing

What is Real Estate Investing?

In **Zero to Hero in Real Estate: The Ultimate Guide for the Over-40 Investor,** we explore the realm of real estate investing, a field rich with potential for those embarking on this venture in their ladder years. Real estate investing encompasses the acquisition, management, and sale or lease of properties for profit, presenting a diverse array of opportunities for wealth creation and financial security.

At its core, real estate investing involves a variety of property types, each with unique characteristics and potential. Residential properties, ranging from single-family homes to multi-unit apartments, offer avenues for rental income and long-term value appreciation. Commercial properties, including office spaces and retail locations, provide opportunities for higher rental yields and longer lease terms, but require a deeper understanding of market dynamics.

Location is a pivotal factor in the success of a real estate investment. Properties in areas with robust economic growth, access to amenities, and positive development trends are more likely to appreciate in value and attract quality tenants. For example, investing in a property in an emerging neighborhood with planned infrastructure can be a strategic move for long-term growth.

Financing these investments is a critical aspect that demands careful consideration. Options range from traditional mortgages to innovative financing methods like REITs or leveraging existing assets. Understanding and choosing the right financing strategy is essential to align with your personal financial goals and risk tolerance.

Managing risks is integral to real estate investing. Market volatility, property devaluation, and operational challenges like tenant management and maintenance are inherent risks that require strategic planning and mitigation.

However, beyond the practicalities, real estate investing is also a journey of personal growth. It challenges individuals to see beyond the immediate, to envision potential where others see barriers, and to cultivate resilience and adaptability. Successful real estate investors combine knowledge with a mindset of perseverance and continuous learning.

Real estate investing over 40 is not just a financial endeavor but a transformative experience. It offers a unique blend of challenges and rewards, demanding both strategic decisions, sound judgment and personal growth. This venture, embarked with knowledge and a visionary mindset, can lead to substantial rewards and payoffs.

Types of Real Estate Investments

Real Estate comes in all shapes and sizes and as a real estate investor, it is wise to know the playing field. It is always good to know the game you are playing. Let's delve into the diverse types of real estate investing. Each potential investment offers unique opportunities and challenges. Understanding these various forms is crucial for developing a strategy that aligns with your personal goals and risk tolerance.

Residential Real Estate Investing involves properties where people live, from single-family homes, townhouses, condominiums, duplexes, triplexes, and quads, to large apartment complexes. What makes these real estate investments appealing is the constant demand for housing. People will always need a place to live, right? As an investor starting out, you could consider a small duplex in a suburban area—you could live in one unit while renting out the other, thereby reducing your living expenses and generating income. Alternatively, investing in a multi-family property in a high-demand urban area could yield substantial rental income as well, though it requires more involved property management.

Commercial Real Estate Investing encompasses properties used for business purposes, such as office buildings, retail spaces, and warehouses. These investments often involve longer lease agreements and can offer more stability in rental income compared to residential properties. For example, owning a small strip mall with diverse tenants—from a coffee shop to a hair salon—can provide a steady income stream, but it also requires a thorough understanding of the dynamics of commercial leasing and tenant needs.

Industrial Real Estate Investing is a niche but potentially lucrative area, focusing on properties used for industrial purposes, like factories, warehouses, and distribution centers. These properties are typically zoned and located outside urban areas and may involve long-term leases with tenants who require specific types of spaces. An example is investing in a warehouse near a transportation hub, which could be attractive to logistics companies.

Retail Real Estate Investing involves properties where goods and services are sold, from small shops to large shopping centers. Retail properties can be sensitive to economic changes but offer opportunities for high foot traffic and visibility. Owning a well-located retail space, perhaps in a busy downtown area or near a popular attraction, can attract high-quality tenants and provide a significant return.

Mixed-Use Real Estate Investing combines residential, commercial, and sometimes industrial spaces within a single property. This type of investment can diversify income sources and reduce risk. A mixed-use property may be in an urban area, with retail shops on the ground floor and apartments above. This is just one example of how you can cater to different tenants' needs while maximizing a good portion of a property's space.

Real Estate Investment Trusts (REITs) offer a way to invest in real estate without owning physical properties. REITs are companies that own, operate, or finance income-generating real estate. Investing in a REIT is similar to buying stocks, providing exposure to real estate with the liquidity of a publicly traded asset. For those who prefer a hands-off approach or want to diversify across various property types and locations, REITs can be an attractive option. It's also one of the easiest ways to begin investing in real estate due to its low upfront capital requirement.

Real Estate Crowdfunding is a newer form of investing, allowing multiple investors to pool their resources to invest in property projects. This method can provide access to higher-value projects with potentially higher returns but also comes with risks, including lack of control over the investment and reliance on the platform's management.

Land Investment is an often-overlooked but significant area of real estate investing. It involves purchasing undeveloped land with the potential for appreciation or development. Land investment requires a visionary approach, foreseeing the future potential of a location. For instance, investing in a piece of land in a rapidly growing suburb can yield substantial returns if the area develops as predicted. This type of investment requires patience and a long-term perspective, but can be less intensive in terms of management compared to developed properties.

Vacation Rental Investing focuses on properties in tourist destinations or popular getaway spots. These properties can generate higher rental income due to their desirable locations and short-term rental potential. An example would be owning a beachfront condo that can be rented out to vacationers. While the income can be substantial, this type of investment requires active management, marketing skills, and an understanding of the tourism market in that area. Airbnb has been a game changer in this space.

Real Estate Syndication is a collaborative investment strategy where investors pool their funds to purchase and manage a property. This approach allows individuals to participate in larger real estate investments with less capital. For example, joining a syndicate to invest in a large commercial building or a high-end residential development. This method offers access to more significant investment opportunities but also requires trust in the syndicate's management and a willingness to share control.

Senior Housing and Assisted Living Investing focuses on properties designed to meet the needs of the aging population. This sector includes retirement communities, assisted living facilities, and nursing homes. Investing in senior housing can be both financially rewarding and socially impactful, as it addresses a growing demographic need. For example, owning a part of an assisted living facility in an area with an aging population presents an opportunity for stable, long-term returns, given the increasing demand for such services.

Student Housing Investing involves properties near colleges and universities catering to the student population. This type of investment can offer high rental demand and resilience during economic downturns. A practical example would be purchasing a multi-unit property near a university to rent to students. While student housing can provide consistent rental income, it also requires an understanding of the unique needs and turnover rates of student tenants.

Real Estate Notes Investing is an alternative way to invest in real estate without owning physical property. It involves purchasing the debt secured by real estate, essentially becoming the lender. For instance, buying a real estate note means you collect the mortgage payments from the borrower. This type of investment can offer a steady income stream and is less management-intensive than owning rental properties, but it requires an understanding of the lending process and risk assessment.

Mobile Home Park Investing involves purchasing and managing a park where individuals own or rent mobile homes. This type of investment can offer high cash flow and lower maintenance costs compared to traditional residential properties. For instance, owning a mobile home park in a region with affordable housing shortages can be a lucrative venture. This investment type requires an understanding of the mobile home market and tenant management, but can be a stable source of income due to the demand for affordable housing options.

Storage Unit Investing focuses on properties dedicated to personal and commercial storage. This niche market has grown in popularity due to the increasing need for storage space. Investing in a well-located storage facility can provide steady rental income with relatively low overhead costs. For example, a storage unit facility near a bustling urban area or a region with high residential turnover can be a profitable investment, especially as these locations often face space constraints.

Real Estate Development involves purchasing land or property to develop or renovate and then sell or lease at a higher value. This type of investment can be highly rewarding, but also carries significant risks and requires substantial capital and expertise. An example is buying a plot of land and developing it into residential units or commercial spaces. Real estate development demands a deep understanding of market trends, construction processes, and project management, but can offer significant returns on investment.

Each of these investment types opens up new possibilities for those starting their real estate journey after 40. Whether it's catering to the needs of senior citizens, providing housing for students, or stepping into the role of a lender, these avenues offer unique ways to engage with the real estate market. They not only diversify your investment portfolio but also allow you to make a meaningful impact in various communities, illustrating that real estate investing can be both a path to personal wealth and a means to contribute positively to society. That sounds like the making of a Hero to me!

Advantages and Risks of Real Estate Investing

In the realm of real estate investing, understanding the balance between advantages and risks is crucial for making informed decisions, especially for those starting at the beginning or later in life. Real estate offers numerous benefits, but it also comes with inherent risks that must be carefully managed. This is one aspect of risk management.

One of the primary advantages of real estate investing is the potential for generating passive income. This can be achieved through rental properties, where the income from tenants can provide a steady cash flow. For example, purchasing a multi-family property in a high-demand area can offer consistent rental income, contributing significantly to your financial stability and growth.

Another advantage is the appreciation of property value over time. Real estate generally increases in value, offering investors the opportunity for long-term wealth accumulation. Consider an investor who bought a property in an emerging neighborhood; over time, as the area develops, the value of the property could significantly increase, resulting in substantial capital gains upon sale.

Real estate also offers tax benefits, such as deductions for mortgage interest, property taxes, operating expenses, and depreciation. These deductions can reduce taxable income, providing a financial advantage to investors. For instance, owning a rental property allows you to deduct expenses related to its maintenance and management, reducing your overall tax burden.

Diversification is another key advantage. By investing in real estate, you can diversify your investment portfolio, reducing reliance on any single asset class. This diversification can help mitigate overall investment risk.

However, real estate investing also carries risks. Market volatility is one such risk. Property values and rental rates can fluctuate due to economic conditions, changes in supply and demand, and other external factors. An investor who purchases a property during a market high may find its value decreasing in a downturn.

Another risk is the potential for negative cash flow. If expenses, such as mortgage payments, maintenance costs, and taxes, exceed the income generated from the property, the investor may face financial strain. For example, if a rental property remains vacant for an extended period, or if significant repairs are needed, it could lead to negative cash flow.

Property management challenges are also a risk. Effective management of rental properties requires time, effort, and knowledge. Dealing with tenant issues, maintenance, and legalities can be demanding. An investor unprepared for these responsibilities may encounter difficulties. If you are not up for the responsibilities of managing properties, one thing to consider is hiring a management company, but be careful, all management companies are not created equal.

Liquidity is another consideration. Real estate is not as liquid as other investments like stocks or bonds. Selling a property can take time, and the process can be complex and costly. This lack of liquidity means that real estate investments may not be suitable for those needing quick access to their funds.

In summary, real estate investing offers a range of advantages. However, it also comes with risks, such as market volatility, negative cash flow, property management challenges, and liquidity concerns. Understanding and balancing these advantages and risks is key to your success in real estate investing, particularly for those embarking on this journey for the very first time or after 40. The good news is, with careful planning, knowledge, and strategy, real estate can be a powerful tool for achieving financial security and growth.

CHAPTER 2

Getting Started with Real Estate Investing

Assessing Your Financial Readiness

In this chapter, we emphasize the importance of a meticulous financial evaluation as the cornerstone of being a successful real estate investor. This process is particularly vital for those embarking on this path later in life, as it sets the foundation for informed and strategic decision-making.

The assessment begins with a comprehensive analysis of your current financial health. This encompasses a thorough review of your income, expenses, debt levels, and savings. This exercise is not just about numbers; it's about gaining a clear and honest understanding of your financial capabilities and constraints. For instance, a robust savings account and manageable debt may signal a readiness to invest, whereas significant financial obligations may signal a lack of readiness to invest. You will have to focus on paying down some debt first.

Creditworthiness plays a crucial role in real estate investing. A high credit score can unlock favorable financing options, impacting the overall cost and feasibility of your investments. Improving or maintaining a strong credit score is, therefore, a proactive step towards enhancing your investment potential.

Savings and emergency funds are another critical aspect. Real estate investing often requires significant initial capital unless you are starting out with some of the other types of investment where you would need little capital to start such as REITs or Wholesaling. Ensuring that you have adequate funds for investment-related expenses while maintaining a separate emergency reserve is crucial for balancing investment aspirations with personal financial security.

Setting clear investment goals aligned with your financial situation and stage of life is imperative.

Whether seeking stable, long-term income or higher-risk, higher-return ventures, your goals should reflect your financial capacity and risk tolerance. This alignment is key to pursuing real estate strategies that resonate with your unique financial landscape and aspirations.

A well-crafted financial plan for your real estate ventures is essential. This plan should encompass a budget, funding strategies, and return projections. It serves as a strategic guide, directing your investment journey towards calculated and realistic outcomes. No investor should ever overlook this step.

Finally, financial education in real estate investing is paramount. Understanding financing mechanisms, tax implications, and cash flow management empowers you with the knowledge to navigate the complexities of real estate investing confidently. As a real estate investor, it is important that you continue learning. Seek out podcasts, online courses, books like this one, attend seminars, join local real estate groups, or hire a coach.

Building Your TEAM of Avengers (Lawyers, Accountants, Real Estate Agents, and Brokers)

The idea of "Building Your TEAM of Avengers" emphasizes the importance of assembling a team of specialized professionals to navigate the intricacies of real estate investing. This team, consisting of lawyers, accountants, real estate agents, and brokers, is essential for informed decision-making and strategic planning.

A real estate lawyer is crucial for legal guidance and protection. They ensure that your transactions comply with laws and regulations, handling contracts and property rights issues. For instance, a lawyer can scrutinize a purchase agreement, safeguarding your interests and ensuring a smooth transaction. Selecting a lawyer with a strong background in real estate law is imperative.

An accountant with real estate expertise is invaluable for financial management and tax planning. They provide insights into the tax implications of your investments and help optimize your financial strategy. A competent accountant can identify tax advantages, advise on investment structures, and enhance your overall financial performance.

Real estate agents and brokers offer market insights and access to investment opportunities. Their knowledge of market trends, property values, and local dynamics is instrumental in identifying lucrative investments. An experienced agent can pinpoint properties that align with your goals and assist in negotiations, giving you an edge in the market.

Mortgage brokers are key in securing the best financing options. They tailor mortgage solutions to your financial situation, helping you navigate the diverse range of available products. A skilled broker ensures that you have access to competitive financing, crucial for maximizing your investment potential.

Building this team requires careful selection and vetting. Seek referrals, conduct interviews, and choose professionals who not only possess expertise in their fields but also share your investment vision and values.

In essence, "Building Your TEAM of Avengers" is about more than just assembling a group of experts;

it's about creating a synergistic team that propels your real estate journey forward. This team becomes your foundation, providing the knowledge, guidance, and support necessary to transition from a novice to a seasoned real estate Hero. With this team by your side, you are equipped to tackle the challenges of real estate investing, turning aspirations into achievements.

Learning the Basics: Terminology and Concepts

In this section, we delve into the essential language and principles of real estate investing. This foundational knowledge is crucial for navigating the complexities of the real estate market, having meaningful conversation and making informed decisions.

Understanding key real estate terminology is the first step in demystifying this real estate investment landscape. Terms like "amortization," the gradual reduction of a loan through regular payments, and "equity," the value of ownership in a property, are vital for comprehending financial structures and the true worth of your investments. These terms are not just jargon; they are tools for deeper understanding and the doorway to opening up the world of real estate investing.

For first-time real estate investors embarking on their journey, understanding key terminology is essential. Although there are many, here are 20 important terms to get you started. Each term is also accompanied by an example to provide clarity and insight into the world of real estate investing:

1. **Amortization**: The process of paying off a loan through structured payments over time. For example, a 30-year fixed-rate mortgage is typically amortized over 30 years, gradually reducing the principal and interest balance.

2. **Cash Flow**: The net income generated from a property after accounting for all expenses. If a rental property earns $2,000 monthly in rent and incurs $1,500 in expenses, the cash flow is $500.

3. **Equity**: The difference between the property's current market value and the remaining mortgage balance. If a property is worth $300,000 and the mortgage owed is $200,000, the equity is $100,000.

4. **Capitalization Rate (Cap Rate)**: A metric used to evaluate the return on an investment property, calculated by dividing the Net Operating

Income (NOI) by the property's value. A property with an NOI of $10,000 and valued at $100,000 has a cap rate of 10%.

5. **Leverage**: Using borrowed capital to increase the potential return of an investment. Buying a $250,000 property with a $50,000 down payment and a $200,000 mortgage is an example of using leverage.

6. **Net Operating Income (NOI)**: The total income from a property minus operating expenses. If a property generates $120,000 annually in rent and has $20,000 in expenses, the NOI is $100,000.

7. **Return on Investment (ROI)**: A measure of the profitability of an investment, calculated by dividing the net profit by the investment's cost. If you invest $100,000 in a property and earn $10,000 annually, your ROI is 10%.

8. **Vacancy Rate**: The percentage of all available units in a rental property that is vacant. A 10-unit building with one unoccupied unit has a vacancy rate of 10%.

9. **1031 Exchange**: A tax-deferred exchange allowing investors to sell a property and reinvest the proceeds in a new property while deferring capital gains taxes. Selling a rental property for $300,000 and

reinvesting in a $500,000 property without immediate tax liability is an example.

10. **Due Diligence**: The process of thoroughly researching a property before purchase. This includes evaluating the physical condition, reviewing financial documents, and assessing legal compliances.

11. **Fixed-Rate Mortgage**: A mortgage with a constant interest rate throughout the entire term. For example, a 30-year fixed-rate mortgage at 4% interest means the interest rate will not change for the duration of the loan.

12. **Adjustable-Rate Mortgage (ARM)**: A mortgage with an interest rate that changes periodically based on a benchmark. An ARM might start with a 3% interest rate for the first five years before adjusting annually.

13. **Pre-Approval**: A lender's conditional commitment to lend a specific amount based on an initial review of the borrower's financial information. For instance, receiving a pre-approval letter for a $250,000 loan helps in house hunting.

14. **Closing Costs**: Fees and expenses paid at the closing of a real estate transaction. This can include

appraisal fees, title insurance, and loan origination fees, typically ranging from 2% to 5% of the purchase price.

15. **Escrow**: A neutral third party holds funds or assets until the completion of a specific condition or event in a real estate transaction. For example, earnest money is often held in escrow until closing.

16. **Real Estate Owned (REO)**: Property owned by a lender, typically a bank, after an unsuccessful foreclosure auction. An REO property is often considered a potential deal for investors since banks may want to remove it from their books.

17. **House Hacking**: A strategy where an investor lives in one unit of a multi-unit property and rents out the others. For instance, buying a duplex, living in one unit, and renting the other can offset your living expenses.

18. **Wholesaling**: A real estate strategy involving a contract with a seller and then transferring that contract to an end buyer for a profit. An investor might secure a property contract for $100,000 and sell it to another investor for $110,000.

19. **Depreciation Recapture**: A tax provision where the IRS collects taxes on the depreciation

claimed on a property when it's sold. For example, if you claimed $50,000 in depreciation and sold the property, you might owe taxes on that $50,000.

20. **Loan-to-Value Ratio (LTV)**: A metric used by lenders to assess lending risk, calculated by dividing the mortgage amount by the property's appraised value. A $180,000 loan on a $200,000 property results in a 90% LTV ratio.

In summary, these additional terms will enrich your real estate vocabulary. It will empower you with the language and concepts necessary for successful real estate investing. Understanding these terms helps in making informed decisions, evaluating opportunities, and navigating the complexities of the real estate market with greater confidence and clarity.

This chapter is not just about financial preparation and fancy vocabulary words, but about setting the stage for a journey that is as financially sound as it is personally fulfilling. Equipped with this newfound knowledge, you, the investor, will be able to approach real estate investing with confidence, wisdom, and insight as well as foresight.

CHAPTER 3

Market Analysis and Location Section

How to Analyze Real Estate Markets

In this chapter, we delve into the critical process of market analysis, an essential skill for any aspiring real estate investor. This chapter provides a structured approach to understanding market dynamics, enabling you to make well-informed investment decisions.

The first step in market analysis is assessing local economic trends. This involves examining indicators such as population growth, employment rates, and economic development. For instance, a city experiencing significant job growth in high-demand sectors may present a robust market for real estate investing. Staying attuned to local economic conditions provides a foundation for predicting market potential.

Understanding supply and demand in the real estate market is crucial. Evaluating the balance between available properties and buyer or renter demand helps in identifying market conditions. A market with low supply and high demand often leads to increased property values, presenting an opportunity for capital appreciation.

Historical price and rental trends offer insights into a market's stability and growth trajectory. Markets with a consistent record of price appreciation and strong rental demand suggest resilience and potential for long-term growth. Analyzing historical data helps forecast future trends and assess investment viability.

Neighborhood characteristics, including quality of schools, crime rates, and access to amenities, significantly influence property values. Properties in neighborhoods with favorable features tend to attract higher prices and rents. For instance, a property near good schools or major employment centers is likely to be more desirable and profitable.

The impact of zoning and future development plans cannot be overstated. Upcoming infrastructure or commercial developments can transform a market, creating new investment opportunities. Being informed about such plans allows you to anticipate market shifts and capitalize on growth potential.

For rental property investors, understanding the local rental market is vital. Researching rental rates, tenant demographics, and occupancy trends provides a picture of rental demand and potential income. A strong rental market with high occupancy rates indicates a sound investment environment.

Finally, consider market-specific risks, such as environmental vulnerabilities or economic dependencies. These are all important for a comprehensive analysis. Markets with higher risk factors may require more cautious investment strategies.

Location - Location - Location: The Importance of Location in Real Estate

With no doubt, location has a profound impact on an investment property. It is the location of a property that will play a critical role in determining the success and value of real estate investments. This chapter provides a focused and insightful exploration of the factors that make location a key determinant in deciding whether to move forward with your real estate investment.

First up, let's talk about the local economy where the future investment property is located. When it comes to the local economy's strength, it is this primary indicator of a property's true potential. A robust economy with diverse employment opportunities suggests a stable real estate market. For instance, investing in a property in a city with a growing job market is likely to yield positive returns due to increased demand for housing. Knowing this now, I am sure you can imagine the impact of a non robust economy in that area.

As a real estate investor, it is also important to look at demographic trends within a neighborhood. Demographic trends will offer valuable insights into market demand. Areas attracting young professionals or families often experience a surge in housing needs, impacting property values and rental rates. Recognizing these demographic shifts can guide investors toward profitable opportunities.

The quality of schools significantly influences residential property values. Homes in districts with top-rated schools tend to command higher prices and rents, appealing to families prioritizing education. Properties in such areas are not only sound investments but also tend to maintain their value in fluctuating markets.

Another area to consider is the accessibility to amenities and transportation, which enhances a property's appeal. Properties close to public transit, shopping, dining, and recreational areas are more attractive to buyers and renters, often leading to higher property values. For example, a home near a subway station or a commercial center is likely to be in higher demand.

Future development plans can transform the landscape of a location as well, creating new investment opportunities. Staying informed about upcoming projects, such as infrastructure improvements or commercial expansions, can help investors capitalize on emerging markets.

Always be on the lookout for safety and crime rates in an area. This is crucial, as they directly affect a property's desirability and value. Properties in safer neighborhoods are generally more sought-after and generally more expensive while maintaining their value, making them wise investment choices.

Cultural and lifestyle factors also play a role in shaping the appeal of a location. Areas known for their cultural vibrancy, scenic beauty, or recreational offerings can attract specific market segments, influencing property demand.

In summary, "Location - Location - Location: The Importance of Location in Real Estate" underscores the centrality of location in real estate investing. By carefully evaluating aspects such as the local economy, demographics, school quality, amenities, future development, crime, and lifestyle, you can determine whether a location is optimal. As an investor armed with this knowledge and information, you are able to feel a bit more comfortable in your decision making when considering investing in a property. Understanding the power of location is not merely about property selection; it's about harnessing opportunity and foresight to see beyond buildings and structures.

Identifying Emerging Markets

Identifying emerging markets is a skill and time and time again it will pay off big if done right. This chapter provides a comprehensive guide to recognizing and capitalizing on the potential of these dynamic markets, offering a path to significant returns and portfolio enhancement.

Emerging markets are characterized by their transformative growth, often driven by economic expansion, infrastructural developments, and increasing housing demand. Identifying these markets requires astute analysis of key indicators and trends.

Economic indicators, such as job growth, population increase, and rising income levels, are the primary markers of an emerging market. Areas experiencing substantial job creation, particularly in stable and growing sectors, indicate robust housing demand. Moreover, population growth, especially among demographics like young professionals and families, suggests a burgeoning need for residential properties.

Infrastructure development is a catalyst for market transformation. New transportation projects, for example, can significantly enhance an area's accessibility and desirability. A suburb benefiting from a new commuter rail link to a city center is a prime example of how infrastructure can spur market demand and growth.

Urban revitalization and redevelopment projects are also indicative of emerging markets. The conversion of underutilized areas, such as industrial zones into mixed-use spaces, often leads to increased property values and investment opportunities. These projects signal a market's potential for growth and profitability.

Analyzing real estate data and trends is crucial in pinpointing emerging markets. Early signs of growth, such as gradual increases in property prices, rental rates, and construction activities, can be key indicators. Leveraging real estate analytics platforms can yield valuable insights into these evolving trends.

Engaging with local real estate professionals provides a wealth of on-the-ground knowledge. Agents, brokers, and fellow investors often possess firsthand information about local developments and market dynamics.

Government policies and incentives can significantly influence the emergence of a market. Areas benefiting from favorable real estate policies, tax incentives, or public amenity investments may attract more residents and investors, stimulating market growth.

In summary, "How to Analyze Real Estate Markets" equips you with the tools to conduct thorough market evaluations, blending academic rigor with practical application. This chapter inspires you to approach real estate investing with a strategic mindset, empowering you with the knowledge to identify promising markets, assess risks, and make decisions that align with your investment goals. Through this analytical lens, you can navigate the rewarding world of real estate with even more confidence and insight.

CHAPTER 4

Financial Fundamentals

Understanding Financial Options

In this chapter, we will dive into a comprehensive overview of the diverse financing methods available for real estate investing. This chapter is designed to equip investors with the knowledge needed to navigate the financial landscape of real estate. It is meant to empower you to make smart decisions that align with your investment objectives.

Traditional mortgages are a cornerstone of real estate financing. They come in various forms, including fixed-rate, adjustable-rate, and interest-only loans. Understanding the nuances of these mortgages, from interest rates to repayment terms, is crucial in selecting the right loan for your investment needs. For example, a 30-year fixed-rate mortgage offers stability in payments, making it a suitable option for long-term investments.

Government-backed loans, such as FHA and VA loans, provide accessible financing options with benefits, like lower down payments and flexible credit requirements. These loans can be particularly advantageous for investors looking to enter the real estate market with limited initial capital.

Hard money loans are an alternative for short-term financing needs, especially in renovation or flipping projects. These loans, sourced from private lenders, are tailored for quick funding and short-duration projects, albeit at higher interest rates.

Creative financing strategies, including seller financing and lease options, offer innovative ways to acquire property. Seller financing, where the seller extends credit to the buyer, and lease options, which combine renting with the option to buy, provide flexible pathways to property ownership without traditional bank financing.

Real Estate Investment Trusts (REIT's) and crowdfunding represent modern approaches to real estate investing. REITs allow investors to buy shares in companies that own and manage properties, providing exposure to real estate with the liquidity of stock investments. Crowdfunding pools resources from multiple investors to fund larger projects, allowing you access to significant real estate ventures.

Basic Financial Calculations (ROI, Cash Flow, Cap Rate, Cash on Cash Return)

As every seasoned investor will ever tell you, "numbers don't lie." I couldn't agree more. It is all in the numbers. Knowing the numbers is everything in real estate investing. You can never afford to put this off and you have to be very meticulous about it. There is no other way! The numbers will give you the x-ray vision, that super power to look into a property to see if you should even bother to invest in the first place. With knowing the numbers, you can calculate your profit and loss, and even be shown the likelihood of a return on your investment (ROI). Sounds exciting, doesn't it? It is so good that even millionaire investors use it. Now let's take a peek into the world of real estate numbers.

Return on Investment (ROI) is a critical measure of an investment's effectiveness. It's calculated by dividing the net profit by the investment's cost. For instance, a property purchased for $200,000 and sold for $250,000, yielding a $50,000 profit, results in an ROI of 25%. ROI serves as a comparative tool to gauge an investment's profitability against other opportunities.

Cash Flow is the net income from a property after all expenses, including mortgage payments. Positive cash flow indicates a property is financially sustainable. Consider a rental property generating $2,000 monthly in rent with $1,500 in expenses, resulting in a $500 monthly cash flow. This metric is vital for ensuring the property contributes positively to your financial goals.

Capitalization Rate (Cap Rate) assesses the return potential of an investment property, useful for comparison. Calculated by dividing the Net Operating Income (NOI) by the property's value, it reflects the risk and return profile. A property with a $20,000 NOI and valued at $200,000 has a cap rate of 10%, providing insight into its investment attractiveness.

Cash on Cash Return focuses on the return on the actual cash invested, especially relevant to leveraged investments. For example, a $50,000 down payment on a property that generates $5,000 annual cash flow has a 10% cash on cash return. This metric offers a precise view of profitability based on the cash invested.

"Basic Financial Calculations (ROI, Cash Flow, Cap Rate, Cash on Cash Return)" equips investors with key tools for financial analysis in real estate. These metrics are more than calculations; they are the lenses through which investment health and potential are viewed. Mastering these calculations empowers investors to make informed, strategic decisions, paving the way for successful real estate ventures.

Next, as an added BONUS, I have added the knowledge of Net Operating Income and the importance of knowing those numbers when it comes to your real estate investment.

Net Operating Income

When it comes to investing into future properties, it is of utmost importance to understand the inner workings of how Net Operating Income works. I want to provide you with an in-depth analysis of NOI, emphasizing its importance as a fundamental metric for evaluating property performance and guiding investment decisions.

NOI is the income generated from a property after deducting all necessary operating expenses but before accounting for financing and taxes. It serves as a pure indicator of a property's operational profitability. Calculating NOI involves subtracting expenses like management fees, maintenance, insurance, and utilities from the total rental income. For instance, a property yielding $120,000 in annual rent with $30,000 in operating expenses results in an NOI of $90,000.

NOI plays a pivotal role in property valuation, particularly when using the Capitalization Rate (Cap Rate) method. The property's value can be estimated by dividing its NOI by the cap rate. For example, an NOI of $90,000 with a 7% cap rate suggests a property value of around $1.29 million or $1,285,714.

Regular assessment of NOI allows investors to track a property's financial health over time. Monitoring changes in NOI helps evaluate the impact of management decisions and market conditions. For example, an increasing NOI over several years can signify effective property management and strategic rent adjustments.

Lenders often use NOI to evaluate a property's ability to service debt, making it a crucial factor in securing financing. A strong NOI can lead to favorable loan terms, such as lower interest rates or higher loan amounts.

While NOI is an essential measure of profitability, it's important to remember that it does not include capital expenditures (CapEx). These are investments in the property's long-term value and should be considered separately from day-to-day operating costs. Understanding and effectively utilizing NOI is more than a financial exercise; it's a strategy for maximizing the potential of your future investments.

With that now in your utility belt, let's look at another very important matter: Budgeting and Financial Planning.

Budgeting and Financial Planning for Real Estate Investments

Focusing on the budgeting and financial planning aspect will have you delve into the essential practices of managing finances effectively for real estate success. This segment combines academic rigor with practical wisdom, guiding you through the nuances of financial stewardship in real estate investing.

The cornerstone of financial planning in real estate is establishing a well-defined budget. This step entails assessing your available resources, including savings and liquid assets, to determine the investment amount. For instance, allocating $30,000 from a $50,000 savings pool sets a clear financial boundary and ensures investments are within your means.

Comprehending the full spectrum of investment-related costs is vital. Beyond the property's purchase price, you must account for closing costs, renovation expenses, ongoing maintenance, property taxes, and insurance. An all-encompassing cost analysis, like factoring in renovation costs to the property purchase price, provides a realistic picture of total investment outlay.

Creating a reserve fund for unforeseen expenses is a prudent financial practice. This fund acts as a buffer for unexpected situations, such as emergency repairs or tenant vacancies, ensuring financial stability. A contingency fund, typically around 10% of the property value, can safeguard against these unpredictable expenses.

Developing a long-term financial plan is integral to achieving your investment objectives. This plan should articulate your goals, whether income generation or capital appreciation, and outline strategies for their realization. For instance, a plan focused on rental income should detail the approach for acquiring and managing rental properties over time.

Regular financial reviews and adjustments are necessary to adapt to changing market conditions and personal financial situations. Staying attuned to market dynamics and being responsive to shifts in your financial circumstances ensures that you continue to make intelligent investment decisions.

CHAPTER 5

The Trinity Approach to Real Estate Valuation

The Sales Comparison Approach

In this chapter, we explore a fundamental technique in real estate valuation, providing a detailed and practical guide to mastering this method. This approach is a cornerstone of property appraisal, relying on comparing the subject property to similar recently sold properties in the same area.

The essence of the Sales Comparison Approach is the principle that a property's value is influenced by the prices of comparable properties, or "comps." Selecting the right comps is critical; they should be similar in key aspects like size, location, and features, and have been sold recently. For example, valuing a four-bedroom house requires finding recent sales of similar four-bedroom houses in the same locality.

Adjustments are often necessary to account for differences between the subject property and the comps. These adjustments could be for factors like property age, size, renovations, and unique features. For instance, if a comp has a swimming pool and the subject property does not, adjusting the comp's sale price downwards provides a more accurate comparison.

Market trends play a significant role in the Sales Comparison Approach. Understanding whether the market is rising or declining is crucial for making appropriate adjustments to the comp prices. In a rising market, a property sold several months ago might be adjusted upwards to reflect current values.

Using multiple comps in the analysis enhances the reliability of the valuation. Averaging the adjusted prices of several comps can provide a more balanced and accurate value estimation, minimizing the impact of any single outlier.

It is highly recommended to thoroughly document and research similar houses you find in the Sales

Comparison Approach. Keeping detailed records of the selected comps, the adjustments made, and the rationale behind the valuation are essential for accuracy and credibility.

By adeptly applying this approach, investors can gain a deeper understanding of property values, enhancing your ability to identify and capitalize on lucrative investment opportunities.

The Cost Approach

Next, we will explore a fundamental property valuation method, especially pertinent for unique or special-purpose real estate. This approach is predicated on the notion that a property's value is essentially the sum of its land value and the cost to construct a similar property, adjusted for depreciation.

The methodology begins with estimating the cost to construct a replica of the subject property at present-day prices, incorporating materials, labor, and other construction-related expenses. For example, valuing a commercial building would entail calculating the current cost to build an equivalent structure, considering contemporary material and labor costs.

Determining the land value is a key step in this approach. It involves comparing the land of the subject property with similar land parcels that have recently been sold, understanding that the value is significantly influenced by location, zoning, and potential utilization. Land in a prime urban location, for instance, typically holds a higher value than a similar-sized plot in a more remote area.

Depreciation is a crucial component of the Cost Approach. Properties depreciate over time due to physical deterioration, functional obsolescence, and external factors affecting the neighborhood. Assessing depreciation requires a nuanced understanding of these elements and their impact on the property's value.

This approach is particularly valuable for properties where comparable sales data is not readily available, such as churches, schools, or custom facilities. For these properties, reconstruction costs provide a more reliable value indicator than sales comparisons.

Executing the Cost Approach demands meticulous analysis, including staying informed about the local construction market and accurately estimating depreciation. It's a method that requires not just technical understanding but also a deep appreciation of the property's unique characteristics.

The Income Approach

Now let's examine The Income Approach. If you ever wanted to know the earning potential of a property, then The Income Approach may be what you are looking for. The Income Approach is a pivotal valuation method in real estate, particularly suited for income-producing properties. This approach equates a property's value to its ability to generate income, a crucial concept for investors focusing on rental properties or commercial real estate.

The process begins with calculating the Net Operating Income (NOI) of the property, which involves deducting operating expenses from the property's gross income. You remember, right? If not, no worries. Soon, this will all be second nature to you. Here is the example we used earlier in implementing the NOI of an investment property. Remember, calculating NOI involves subtracting expenses like management fees, maintenance, insurance, and utilities from the total rental income. For instance, a property yielding $120,000 in annual rent with $30,000 in operating expenses results in an NOI of $90,000.

Another fundamental property valuation method is determining the capitalization (cap) rate. Determining the appropriate cap rate can be a very beneficial and critical step in determining the property value. This rate reflects the expected rate of return on the investment, informed by market comparisons. If similar properties in the market yield a 7% return ($70,000 NOI on a $1,000,000 value), the cap rate for valuation would be 7%. Another useful way to look at it for investors is from our earlier example, in which the **Capitalization Rate (Cap Rate)** assesses the return potential of an investment property, useful for comparison. The cap rate is calculated by dividing the Net Operating Income (NOI) by the property's value, thus it reflects the risk and return profile. A property with a $20,000 NOI and valued at $200,000 has a cap rate of 10%, providing insight into its investment attractiveness.

The property's value is estimated by dividing the NOI by the cap rate. With a $70,000 NOI and a 7% cap rate, the property's estimated value would be $1,000,000. This calculation is central to understanding what an investor might be willing to pay for the property based on its income generation.

The Income Capitalization Approach is particularly potent for properties like apartment complexes and retail centers, where income generation is a key value driver. It provides a clear framework for assessing investment potential, allowing for comparisons across different properties based on their capacity to generate income.

In summary, this chapter provides a comprehensive and academic exploration of this valuation method, empowering investors with the ability to discern the value of income-producing properties. This approach is more than a financial formula; it's a strategic tool for evaluating the intrinsic worth and income potential of a property, forming the bedrock of sound investment decisions in the realm of real estate. This is powerful stuff!

CHAPTER 6

Real Estate Investment Strategies

REITS Investment Strategy

In this chapter on Real Estate Investment Strategies, we will arm ourselves with the knowledge of Real Estate Investment Trusts, better known as REITs. We will examine their role as an innovative and accessible avenue for real estate investment. This chapter academically explores the structure, benefits, and considerations of REITs, providing insight and guidance for investors seeking to diversify their portfolios.

REITs are entities that own, operate, or finance income-generating real estate. They level the playing field for real estate investors, allowing individuals to participate in the sector without the complexities of direct property ownership. REITs are legally mandated to distribute most of their income as dividends, offering an attractive yield to income-seeking investors.

Trading on major exchanges like stocks, REITs provide liquidity, enabling investors to easily enter and exit positions. This feature allows for flexible investment strategies, similar to stock market investing, but with the added benefit of real estate exposure. For example, investing in a retail REIT provides exposure to commercial real estate's income and growth without the direct burdens of property management and large capital commitments.

Diversification is a hallmark of REITs. Investors gain exposure to a broad array of real estate assets across various sectors and geographies, mitigating the risks associated with individual property investments. This diversification enhances portfolio resilience, spreading risk across multiple properties and market segments.

REITs present a rather easily accessible entry point into real estate investing. They offer a practical solution for those without substantial capital to directly invest in properties, allowing investors to tap into the real estate market's potential with smaller capital outlays.

However, REITs also carry market-related risks. Their stock-like nature subjects them to market volatility, and their performance is influenced by both real estate and broader economic trends. Furthermore, the requirement to distribute most earnings can limit their ability to reinvest and grow capital value.

In summary, REITs provide a comprehensive and academic exploration of Real Estate Investment Trusts, framing them as a strategic and flexible option for real estate investing. This chapter inspires investors to consider REITs as a practical, diversified approach to accessing the real estate market with ease. This should excite any real estate investor looking to get in on the ground floor with very little cash output to get started.

Wholesaling Investment Strategy

Let's turn our attention now to the "Wholesaling Investment Strategy," Wholesaling is a dynamic strategy in real estate investment. This approach involves identifying undervalued properties, securing them under contract, and then assigning the contract to a buyer for a profit, all without taking ownership of the property.

The first phase of wholesaling is rigorous market research. It's essential to understand the local real estate landscape and pinpoint areas where properties are undervalued. This could involve areas poised for growth or neighborhoods where sellers are motivated due to financial or personal reasons. For example, focusing on a community undergoing revitalization can reveal properties with untapped potential.

Finding properties is the next critical step. This includes strategies like direct mail campaigns, engaging with real estate agents, or exploring public records for distressed properties. A successful tactic might involve targeting homeowners in financial distress, signaling your willingness to purchase their property.

Negotiating a favorable contract is pivotal in wholesaling. The contract should allow for an assignment to another buyer and be negotiated at a price that leaves enough margin for profit. For instance, securing a contract to purchase a property for $100,000, which, with minimal repairs, could value at $150,000, presents an opportunity for profit.

Locating a buyer is a crucial phase. This often involves tapping into a network of investors interested in rehab projects or rental properties. Utilizing real estate investment networks and online platforms can facilitate the development of a robust buyer list. One of the easiest strategies is to simply drive around in a desired neighborhood if you find it safe and simply knock on doors.

Assigning the contract to a buyer for a fee constitutes the profit in wholesaling. This fee is the difference between your contracted price and the sale price to the buyer. For example, a property contracted at $100,000 and assigned to a buyer for $110,000 yields a $10,000 profit.

Understanding the legal and ethical aspects of wholesaling is fundamental. Consulting with a real estate attorney ensures the legality of transactions, and maintaining transparency with all parties upholds ethical standards.

In summary, "Wholesaling Investment Strategy" provides a comprehensive and academic exploration of wholesaling, offering insights into market research, property sourcing, negotiation, and legal considerations. This segment should inspire investors to adopt a strategic and ethical approach to real estate investing, emphasizing the importance of diligence, negotiation skills, and integrity in achieving success in the wholesaling arena.

Fix and Flip Strategy

Have you ever wanted to fix and flip houses? The Fix and Flip Investment Strategy may be one of the most dynamic and rewarding real estate investment strategies. In this segment, we will explore the process of purchasing undervalued properties, renovating them, and selling for a profit, offering a blueprint for transforming real estate ventures into lucrative outcomes.

The strategy begins with meticulous property selection. It involves market research to identify properties below market value, offering significant upside potential through renovation. For instance, targeting a home in a desirable neighborhood that requires cosmetic updates can serve as a prime candidate for a successful flip.

Conducting due diligence is paramount. A thorough property inspection to identify structural and aesthetic issues informs the feasibility and budgeting of the project. Identifying key issues, such as an outdated electrical system, ensures informed decision-making and budget planning.

Renovation is the cornerstone of the fix and flip strategy. Developing a clear and cost-effective renovation plan is crucial, focusing on improvements that significantly enhance property value. Strategic renovations might include kitchen updates, bathroom remodels, and curb appeal enhancements, always mindful of budget constraints and market trends.

Financing the project is another critical component. Options range from traditional mortgages to more agile financing like hard money loans. The choice depends on factors such as project timeline, capital availability, and investor risk tolerance. For example, hard money loans can offer quick access to funds but typically come at a higher cost.

The final stage, selling the property, combines strategic pricing with effective marketing. Utilizing professional staging, high-quality photography, and comprehensive market listings can maximize property appeal and sale price. Pricing strategies should balance market competitiveness with the aim of recouping investment and profit.

Fix and Flip Investment Strategy can often have a lot of moving parts and is very double with a little know how. Isn't it inspiring to embrace this strategy not only as a means to profit, but as an opportunity to add value, develop project management skills, and realize the transformative potential of real estate investing? To succeed at this game, you must also develop the eye of seeing potential beyond the mess.

Renting and Leasing Investment Strategy

If you ever imagine being a landlord, then this section is for you. Renting and leasing can propel you into an entirely different world. This chapter provides a high level roadmap for successfully managing rental properties, from property selection to tenant relations and financial management.

The process starts with strategic property selection, considering factors like location, property type, and target tenant demographics. Remember, a property near a university is likely to attract student tenants, while a family home in a suburb appeals to long-term residents.

As an investor, be very careful not to price yourself above or below market. It is important to determine the appropriate rent. Believe me, it is a crucial step. Appropriately pricing your property for rent or lease will require market research to understand local rental rates. Competitive pricing ensures the property is attractive to potential tenants while maximizing income potential. Also, utilizing online rental platforms can offer valuable insights into setting the right rent.

Marketing the property effectively and conducting thorough tenant screening is key to finding suitable tenants. Marketing strategies might include online listings and collaboration with local agents, while screening should encompass credit checks and employment verification to ensure tenant reliability.

Drafting a comprehensive lease agreement is fundamental. The lease should clearly outline all terms and conditions, ensuring both parties understand their rights and responsibilities. Legal compliance in the lease agreement is vital to prevent future disputes and misunderstandings. Here you can call on one of your Avengers, the real estate attorney.

Ongoing property maintenance and management are necessary for preserving the property's value and tenant satisfaction. Regular upkeep, prompt repairs, and possibly employing a property management company are all aspects of effective property management.

Understanding legal obligations and tenants' rights is imperative for a landlord. Awareness of local laws, including safety regulations and eviction procedures, is essential for lawful and ethical property management.

Lastly, robust financial planning and record-keeping are crucial for the business aspect of renting and leasing. This involves budgeting for expenses, monitoring income and expenditures, and preparing for tax obligations. Use your accountant Avenger here. It is important to mention here that efficient financial management underpins the profitability and sustainability of your real estate investment.

Buy and Hold Strategy

Last on the list is "Buy and Hold Investment Strategy." Here we will illuminate a path to achieving enduring financial success through real estate. This strategy, centered on acquiring and retaining properties over time, capitalizes on the transformative power of rental income and property appreciation.

At the heart of this strategy lies the art of razor sharp property selection. It involves a deep dive into market research, identifying areas ripe for growth and resilience. Picture yourself investing in a neighborhood on the cusp of an economic renaissance, where you foresee its future and recognize its potential. This will translate into significant long-term appreciation and a very lucrative outcome.

Finding and securing the right financing is a step that combines wisdom and strategy. Whether it's through a traditional mortgage or more creative financing options, the choice should resonate with your vision of financial growth and stability. Imagine locking in a mortgage with terms that not only fit your current financial situation but also align with your long-term wealth-building goals.

Let us take into account that effective property management emerges as a cornerstone of this strategy. It's about creating lasting value through meticulous tenant selection, proactive property maintenance, and savvy financial and legal management. Envision the peace of mind that comes from knowing your investment is not just preserved, but is thriving under expert stewardship. That is the power of your Avengers TEAM.

Embracing the nuances of tax planning can significantly enhance the profitability of your investments. Turning every allowable deduction to your advantage and strategically planning for future tax implications is surely a win-win and will also maximize your investment's return.

Diversification is the name of the game in your real estate portfolio. By spreading your investments across different property types and locations, you not only mitigate risks, but also create multiple streams of income. Envision a portfolio that weathers market fluctuations and provides consistent returns, putting financial freedom closer in reach.

Regularly revisit and refine your investment strategy based on the response and changes in the markets and your personal goals. That's essential, and it's also about being agile and responsive, seizing opportunities for refinancing or timing property sales to capitalize on market conditions.

"Buy and Hold Investment Strategy" is more than just a chapter; it's a motivational blueprint for transforming your financial future through real estate. It empowers you to embark on a journey of wealth creation, offering the tools and insights to build a robust, income-generating real estate portfolio. This strategy is your gateway to achieving long-term financial success and leaving a lasting legacy in the world of real estate investing.

CHAPTER 7

Risk Management In Real Estate Investing

Identifying Common Risks

In this section we'll explore what is involved in understanding and managing the risks inherent in real estate investing. This chapter provides an academic yet practical analysis of common risks, equipping investors with the knowledge to navigate these challenges effectively and confidently.

Market volatility is a primary risk in real estate. Property values and rental incomes can fluctuate due to economic shifts and market dynamics. For example, an economic downturn can depress property values and rental rates. Awareness of market trends and economic indicators enables investors to anticipate and adapt to these changes.

Negative cash flow is another significant risk. This occurs when a property's expenses exceed its income, potentially leading to financial strain. Sound financial planning, including accurate budgeting and reserve funds, is crucial to avoid this pitfall.

Property management challenges, ranging from tenant relations to maintenance and legal compliance, are common in real estate. Problematic tenants or unexpected repairs can disrupt income and inflate costs. Effective property management, whether through personal oversight or professional services, is key to mitigating risks of this type.

Liquidity risk is inherent in real estate's relatively illiquid nature. The time required to sell a property and access capital can pose challenges, especially in urgent financial situations. Also, diversification and strategic planning are essential to managing risk.

Financing risk, related to mortgages and loans, is affected by interest rate fluctuations and personal financial changes. For example, an increase in interest rates can raise mortgage payments. Securing stable financing and maintaining a robust financial profile are strategies to counter this risk.

Legal and regulatory risks encompass compliance with laws and regulations, including zoning, building codes, and tenant rights. Non-compliance can result in legal issues and financial losses. Staying informed and seeking legal counsel can help navigate these complexities.

In summary, "Identifying Common Risks" offers an insightful and motivational guide to recognizing and addressing the risks in real estate investing. Equipped with this knowledge, you can turn potential obstacles into opportunities for maximum growth and success in the real estate market. Now things are heating up!

Mitigation Strategies

Let's explore this very important topic of "Mitigation Strategies." This chapter will delve into the essential techniques for reducing and managing risks in real estate investing. It also combines academic principles with practical, real-world advice, offering investors strategies to safeguard and maximize their investments.

Diversification is a fundamental risk mitigation strategy. It involves spreading investments across various property types and locations to minimize the impact of market volatility. For example, a portfolio that includes residential, commercial, and industrial properties across different regions provides stability and resilience against market shifts. The name of the game is diversification, diversification, diversification.

Conducting thorough market research and due diligence is vital. This includes analyzing economic trends, demographics, and area-specific developments. Investing in an area with positive growth indicators, such as new infrastructure or increasing population, can reduce the risk of depreciation and vacancy.

Effective financial planning is crucial in mitigating risk. This encompasses setting realistic budgets, maintaining emergency reserves, and prudent cash flow management. For instance, a reserve fund covering several months of property expenses can buffer against unexpected costs, ensuring financial stability.

Insurance is a key element in risk management. Tailoring insurance coverage to the specific needs of each property, including additional policies for properties in high-risk areas, offers protection against unforeseen losses.

Adhering to legal compliance is non-negotiable. Understanding and abiding by zoning laws, building codes, and tenant rights not only prevents legal issues but also enhances the investment's credibility. Regularly updating legal knowledge and seeking professional advice can prevent costly legal entanglements.

Maintaining positive tenant relationships is a strategic mitigation approach. Building rapport with tenants can lead to longer tenancies, lower vacancy rates, and better care for the property. Good communication and responsive property management foster a stable and profitable landlord-tenant dynamic.

Regular property maintenance and inspections are essential for preserving value and preventing significant repairs. Proactive maintenance, such as routine checks and prompt repair work, minimizes the risk of costly damages and prolongs the property's lifespan.

To recap, "Mitigation Strategies" provides a guide to managing risks in real estate investing. It highlights the importance of diversification, research, financial planning, insurance, legal compliance, tenant relations, and property maintenance. This chapter empowers investors to approach real estate with a strategic and proactive mindset, turning potential risks into opportunities for growth and long-term success.

Insurance and Legal Protection

This final chapter provides an academically informed yet practical approach to understanding and implementing insurance and legal strategies to protect your assets and ensure the longevity of your investments.

Insurance plays a pivotal role in real estate investment protection. It's crucial to understand various insurance types, such as landlord insurance, which covers property damage, liability, and potential loss of rental income. In regions prone to specific risks, additional policies like flood or earthquake insurance are vital. Tailoring insurance coverage to each property's unique risks ensures comprehensive protection.

Liability insurance is a key component, safeguarding against legal claims related to injuries or accidents on your property. It provides a financial buffer for legal expenses and potential damages, underscoring the importance of risk management through regular property inspections and maintenance.

A thorough understanding of legal requirements in real estate is indispensable. Familiarity with landlord-tenant laws, zoning regulations, and fair housing acts is crucial to maintaining compliant and ethical investment practices. This knowledge not only prevents legal disputes but also fosters a responsible and respectful investment approach.

Creating a legal entity, such as an LLC, offers an additional layer of protection. It separates personal assets from investment properties, limiting personal liability. This legal structure can be instrumental in safeguarding personal wealth in the face of property-related legal challenges.

Engaging with legal and insurance professionals is a must. Their expertise provides customized guidance and clarity on the specific legal and insurance needs of your real estate portfolio, ensuring that your investments are well-protected and compliant with relevant laws and regulations.

Next Steps In Your Real Estate Investment Journey

Education is your most powerful tool. Where there is knowledge, there is potential power! I say potential power because unless you are in action using it, that knowledge you now hold will have no power. Engaging in lifelong learning keeps you at the forefront of the ever-evolving real estate market. Imagine uncovering a groundbreaking investment strategy at a seminar or through an industry publication, catapulting your portfolio to new heights. Embrace the pursuit of knowledge as an exciting and endless journey.

Building a robust network is like planting seeds for future success. Each connection, whether with seasoned professionals or fellow investors, is a potential source of invaluable insights and opportunities. Envision forming a partnership through a real estate group that leads to a lucrative investment deal—the power of networking can turn possibilities into realities.

Setting clear, ambitious goals is the compass that guides your investment decisions. Whether it's acquiring a diverse range of properties or achieving a specific income milestone, having defined goals provides direction and motivation. Visualize reaching your investment targets and setting new, even more ambitious ones, propelling your journey forward.

Diversification is your safeguard against uncertainty. A well-balanced portfolio across various property types and markets is your armor against market volatility. Picture the stability and confidence that comes from knowing your investments are resilient, capable of weathering economic storms.

Rigorous risk management is your strategy for enduring success. Proactively identifying and mitigating risks ensures that your investments stand the test of time. Imagine the peace of mind that comes from having a comprehensive insurance plan and a solid emergency fund in place.

Adapting your strategy in response to market changes and personal growth keeps your investment journey dynamic and rewarding. Stay flexible and responsive, and be ready to seize new opportunities as they arise. Envision yourself skillfully navigating market shifts, turning challenges into stepping stones for success.

Embrace this journey with enthusiasm, determination, and a burning desire, and watch as your real estate ventures flourish, bringing you closer to your dreams of financial freedom and success.

The Golden Key – Zero to Hero in Real Estate Mindset

I would not be worth my salt if we did not talk about mindset. As a hero of change, educator, and coach, it is my fiduciary responsibility to leave you with the tools that, when applied, get you ready for whatever there is to be ready for.

Imagine, if you will, embarking on an exhilarating path of perpetual learning in real estate. Each piece of knowledge you acquire is a precious gem, enriching your understanding and sharpening your market intuition. Picture yourself attending an industry conference, where a single insight opens the door to an extraordinary investment opportunity, catapulting your portfolio to new heights.

Resilience, your unwavering ally, transforms challenges into stepping stones to success. Visualize navigating a complex property deal, emerging not just victorious but fortified in spirit and expertise. Each obstacle becomes a testament to your growth, building an unshakeable foundation for your future achievements.

Imagine goal-setting and strategic planning become your compass and map. Envision your ambitions vividly—a real estate empire, financial independence, a legacy of success, a HERO. These aren't mere dreams or images; they are concrete goals. They are attainable and they are yours.

For a moment, imagine risk management, where you have honed your skills to perfection, as you become the ultimate problem solver. Imagine what it would be like to master the art of balancing bold moves with calculated caution. Envision confidently navigating market uncertainties, making informed decisions that maximize gains while protecting your investments and protecting your family.

See, in this moment, networking, the lifeblood of your real estate journey, feel yourself connecting to endless possibilities. See yourself forging bonds with industry leaders, mentors, and peers, while each relationship, a mutually beneficial alliance, fuels your journey towards greatness!

Calling you into being is adaptability, your strategic superpower, which empowers you to thrive amidst market fluctuations as you stay agile and responsive, ready to seize emerging opportunities as the market landscape evolves. And as you imagine this, you say to yourself out loud, **"I am a hero, a real estate investor, creating a new path of unwavering confidence, action, strength, knowledge, and know-how. I AM A HERO, MAKING A DIFFERENCE AND I HAVE MORE POWER FOR THE WORLD TO SEE!"**

This mindset technique that I offer you isn't just a key to your real estate success—it is your golden key! This golden key is a transformative force that, once practiced daily with passion and conviction, propels you into your real estate journey with unprecedented power and momentum. Embrace it! Embrace it passionately, act decisively, and witness the extraordinary transformation of what it is to be a

HERO on your real estate journey. Whether you start slow or whether you start small, it doesn't matter. Whatever you do, just START! Your life will never be the same! The time for action is now! Let real estate investing call you into being! Let your greatness and the legacy that you are about to create flourish!